growing tomatoes

growing tomatoes

a directory of varieties and how to cultivate them successfully

Richard Bird and **Christine France**

LORENZ BOOKS

This edition is published by Lorenz Books,
an imprint of Anness Publishing Ltd,
108 Great Russell Street,
London WC1B 3NA;
info@anness.com

www.lorenzbooks.com;
www.annesspublishing.com

If you like the images in this book
and would like to investigate using
them for publishing, promotions or
advertising, please visit our website
www.practicalpictures.com for
more information.

A CIP catalogue record for this book
is available from the British Library.

Publisher: Joanna Lorenz
Senior Editor: Doreen Palamartschuk
Additional Text: Peter McHoy
Variety Photography: Janine Hosegood
Other Photography: Jonathan Buckley
    and Peter Anderson
Jacket Photography: Martin Brigdale
Illustrations: Liz Pepperall
Designers: Paul Calver and Louise Kirby
Production Controller: Rosanna Anness

PUBLISHER'S NOTE
Although the advice and information
in this book are believed to be accurate
and true at the time of going to press,
neither the authors nor the publisher can
accept any legal responsibility or liability
for any errors or omissions that may have
been made nor for any inaccuracies nor
for any loss, harm or injury that comes
about from following instructions or
advice in this book.

Contents

Introduction

Tomatoes are probably the most widely grown of all vegetables. Even people without a garden often manage to grow a plant or two on a balcony, patio or terrace. One reason for this is that tomatoes are relatively easy to grow, another is that home-grown tomatoes have a far superior flavour to shop-bought tomatoes.

There is a huge range of sizes, colours and flavours available, with constant new introductions, while some of the old-fashioned varieties, still recognized as being among the best-flavoured, are becoming more readily available. The largest, such as the beefsteak tomatoes, can weigh up to 450g/1lb each, while the smallest are not much more than the size of grapes.

EARLY HISTORY

The early history of the tomato is not clear, but it is thought that the first tomatoes grew wild in South America, to the west of the Andes in what is now Peru, Bolivia, northern Chile and Ecuador. The ancestors of the Incas and Aztecs were the first to cultivate the tiny, cherry-sized fruits around AD700. By the time the Spaniards conquered Mexico in the early 16th century, tomatoes were widely domesticated there and throughout South America. It is likely to have been an early Spanish explorer, perhaps Christopher Columbus or Hernando Cortés, who brought the tomato to Europe.

NAMING THE TOMATO

The early tomatoes introduced to Europe were small and yellow in colour, not bright red as is common today. They were named Peruvian apples, or, often "golden apples".

Either through their supposed aphrodisiac qualities or because folk medicine linked the appearance of plants to their therapeutic use (tomatoes look very like hearts), they also earned the name of "love apples" or *pommes d'amour,* which may also be a simple corruption of *pomo d'oro.*

The tomato plant is a member of the deadly nightshade family, and the tomato was at first believed to be poisonous. In fact, the fruits are not at all toxic, but the foliage is poisonous, and the leaves can cause bad stomach upsets if eaten.

LEFT In sheltered, sunny gardens tomatoes can be grown in a corner of the vegetable plot.

EARLY CULTIVATION

Tomatoes flourished in the warm climates of Spain and Italy, and these were the first European nations to realize the potential of tomatoes in cooking, using them in recipes from the late 17th century onwards. The early development of new and hardy strains was centred largely around the Mediterranean, and by the mid-18th century there were more than 1,000 tomato varieties, cultivated throughout Spain, Portugal, Italy and the south of France.

Eventually the rest of Europe followed suit, helped greatly by the discovery that tomatoes would flourish in glasshouses, extending their season over months instead of weeks. The first glasshouses in England were built in Kent and Essex in the mid-19th century, when sheet glass production was quite a recent innovation.

It is not certain who was responsible for introducing

tomatoes to North America, but the colonies were surprisingly cautious about them and at first treated them with suspicion when they were brought from Europe in the early 18th century. However, tomatoes were cultivated from the mid-18th century in Carolina, and by the late 1700s the migration of farmers across North America took tomato cultivation north and west and to the central coast of Florida. By the early 19th century tomatoes were widely used in cooking.

THE PRESENT-DAY TOMATO

There are now well over 7,000 varieties, and new hybrids are constantly being introduced, while some older favourites have been brought back into cultivation.

Tomatoes are grown all over the world, from Iceland to New Zealand. They are one of the main horticultural crops of Britain, about 80 per cent being grown in heated

ABOVE If they are left on the vine, tomatoes will continue to ripen after they have been picked.

glasshouses, with the rest of the crop being grown almost entirely in unheated greenhouses.

From the day the flowers appear on the tomato plants, it takes between 40 and 60 days for the fruits to reach their peak of ripeness, depending on the tomato variety. If they are grown in unheated greenhouses the weather will also be a factor. For the finest flavour, tomatoes need to be ripened in the sun and on the vine, and from the first sign of ripening it takes four to six days for a tomato to reach full ripeness.

Commercially, the fruit is picked when it is half-ripened so that it will reach the customer when it is at peak ripeness and to extend its shelf-life. Many tomatoes are now sold on the vine, partly for aesthetic reasons, and partly because it helps them to ripen better and keep a little longer.

LEFT Tomatoes are versatile and combine well with herbs such as basil and garlic.

Potato/Tomato graft

types of
tomato

There are believed to be more than
7,000 different cultivars of tomato,
ranging from those that are specially
hybridized and grown for supermarkets
to old-fashioned, heritage tomatoes.
Whether you want tomatoes to eat raw
in salads or to use in cooked dishes,
and whether you grow them in a
greenhouse or outdoors in your garden,
you will find a tomato to suit every
possible situation and preference.

Guide to tomato types

Nowadays, there is a wider choice of tomatoes available than ever before, both to grow yourself in the garden or greenhouse. They vary enormously in colour, shape and size as well as flavour.

Supermarkets often commission growers to breed tomatoes that fit their requirements exactly, from sweetness and colour to shape and skin thickness. Careful cross-pollination and generations of selective breeding can vary all these factors. This has led to an unusual situation in the fruit and vegetable world: namely that the tomato is one of the few fruits and vegetables that has been branded.

When a supermarket chain commissions a grower to breed a tomato exclusively for sale in their stores, a new, own-brand name is chosen, which does not reveal the tomato's origins, even though it might be a hybrid of a familiar variety.

Home-grown tomatoes have a naturally low water content and so usually have a better flavour and texture than most supermarket tomatoes. Most gardeners will have used organic methods, relying on sustainable growing practices and without the use of pesticides and synthetic fertilizers. Many of the indoor varieties can be grown outside in warmer climates.

ROUND OR SALAD TOMATOES

These tomatoes, which are the most common type available, vary in size according to the exact variety and the time of year. Their flavour varies considerably, depending on whether they are grown and picked during their natural season. They are generally quite acidic with a full flavour, so they are excellent for cooking or eating raw. For cooking, look for fruit that is soft and very red. Add a pinch of sugar to bring out the sweetness and season well with salt and pepper to bring out the flavour.

BEEFSTEAK TOMATOES

These pumpkin-shaped, large and sometimes ridged tomatoes used to be called oxheart tomatoes. They are usually deep red or orange in colour. They have a good firm texture, plenty of flesh and a sweet, mellow flavour due to their low acidity and often high water content. They are good to eat raw, but are often excellent when sliced, grilled or fried.

beefsteak tomatoes

round or salad tomatoes

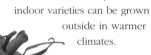

CHERRY TOMATOES

These small, dainty cherry-size tomatoes are mouth-wateringly sweet. High in sugar and low in acid, they are good in salads or for cooking whole. The skin can be very delicate in the summer months, but tends to toughen towards the end of the season. They are perfect as part of a cocktail snack as they are just the right size for one mouthful.

Cherry tomatoes were once prized treasures exclusive to gardeners but they are now widely available. The delicious flavour remarkably improves with keeping. Red, yellow and orange varieties of cherry tomato are available, and among the most popular cultivars are the reliable old favourite 'Gardener's Delight' and the newer, yellow 'Mirabelle'. They look particularly attractive when presented to the table on the vine.

cherry tomatoes

PLUM TOMATOES

These tomatoes are elongated and are usually shaped like an egg, but they are occasionally very long and almost hollow inside. They have a meaty flesh, a thick core, strong skin, which can be easily peeled, and are richly flavoured, with fewer seeds than round tomatoes. They are considered to be the best cooking tomatoes because of their concentrated flavour and high acidity. They are best used when they are fully ripe.

Plum tomatoes are available in various sizes and colours, but red plum tomatoes are best for cooking. They are grown widely in Italy and are the most popular type for canning. In cooler climates, plum tomatoes need to be grown under glass.

PEAR TOMATOES

This small category of tomatoes is pear-shaped and generally quite small. Pear tomatoes include some of the tastiest tomatoes of all, but they are not very widely grown. Perhaps the best-known variety is 'Yellow Pear', a vigorous grower that produces masses of tiny yellow fruits. They look pretty on the

plum tomatoes

plate, and have a mild, citrus flavour. 'Red Pear' tomatoes have a richer flavour and are popular. In tomato tastings, these score highly for flavour.

pear tomatoes

VINE TOMATOES

This term can refer to any variety of tomato that is still attached to the stalk or vine. They have the aromatic quality usually present only in home-grown tomatoes. This is mostly due to the chemicals coming from the green stalk and leaf of the plant, rather than the fruit itself. Rich red vine tomatoes are perfect in salads.

YELLOW TOMATOES

These tomatoes have a sweet, slightly lemony, mild flavour and a lower acidity than red tomatoes. Yellow tomatoes come in different shapes and sizes, from pear to plum and round. Yellow tomatoes should ideally be used in salads and also for garnishes because of their decorative quality, but they are quite suitable for cooking and are especially good in the preparation of pickles and chutneys. The 'Yellow Pear' variety, so called because of the shape, is particularly popular.

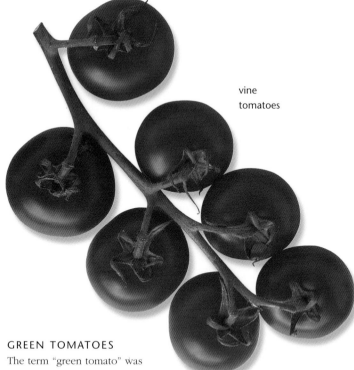

vine
tomatoes

GREEN TOMATOES

The term "green tomato" was used for the tangy, unripened tomatoes traditionally used for relishes and chutneys. Ripe green tomatoes are also available now – for example, the green and yellow cherry tomato 'Green Grape', and the cordons 'Evergreen' and stripy 'Green Zebra'. They have a bright green skin and flesh and are flavoursome and very decorative used in salads and garnishes.

yellow
tomatoes

green
tomato

orange
tomatoes

ORANGE TOMATOES

These mild tomatoes have a sweet,
delicate flavour and low acidity.
Like red, round salad tomatoes,
they have quite a high seed to flesh
ratio. The seeds, however, are often
smaller than in the red tomato.
Orange tomatoes add a splash of
colour to salads, create wonderful
garnishes and are also good in
soups and sauces. 'Orange
Bourgoin' and 'Mini Orange' are
pretty varieties that are easily grown.

GROWTH HABITS

Tomatoes have traditionally been
grown, both in greenhouses and outdoors, as cordons or indeterminates.
These are upright plants supported
on strings or canes from which any
sideshoots, other than fruiting stems,
are removed and the main stem
stopped after four or five trusses.

Bush varieties, also known as
determinates, have become popular

RIGHT Plum tomatoes have a deep red
colour and rich flavour.

in more recent times for growing
outside, as these need less attention
than the cordons in that they need
no support and the sideshoots are
not removed. They make a straggly
bush, which tends to sprawl over
the soil and so needs to be
underlaid with straw to keep the
dirt from the fruit. Slugs can also
be a problem.

Semi-determinate tomatoes are
bushes that are very sprawling and
need some trimming back to keep
them in control. In practice, many
gardeners treat determinates and
semi-determinates in the same way
and just let them sprawl.

Round or salad tomatoes

These are the most commonly grown tomatoes, especially in temperate areas. They are easy to grow and usually produce prolific crops. Their size, in between the bite-size cherry tomatoes and the hefty beefsteaks, makes them useful both in salads and in cooking.

AILSA CRAIG

This tomato was bred by a Scottish grower in Ayrshire, and takes its name from a rocky island in the Firth of Clyde. It is grown both outdoors and under glass. The mid-red fruits are medium-size, about 5cm/2in in diameter, with smooth, thick skin. 'Ailsa Craig' has a good sweet flavour. It is the source of several successful hybrids.

ALICANTE

An early maturing, English cordon-type tomato, 'Alicante' is regarded as a good choice for novice gardeners as it is not difficult to grow and crops very well. The medium-size fruits are uniform, smooth and red, with a very good flavour. 'Alicante' tomatoes remain firm when grilled (broiled), roasted or baked, and are ideal for vegetable kebabs.

ARARAT FLAMED

Bred from a Hungarian variety, 'Debrecen', this good-looking tomato is clearly flamed, with dark green stripes on the skin, which fade as the fruit ripens. It is a cordon type, with a big yield and good flavour.

'Ailsa Craig'

'Alicante'

'Ararat Flamed'

VARIETIES TO GROW INSIDE OR OUTSIDE

Inside (cordon)
'Mirabelle'
'Rosadel'
'Sun Belle'
'Supersweet 100'

Inside or outside (cordon)
'Ailsa Craig'
'Alicante'
'Andine Cornue'
'Ararat Flamed'
'Black Russian'
'Chadwick'
'Flamme'
'Gardener's Delight'
'Golden Sunrise'
'Green Zebra'
'Harbinger'
'Jubilee'
'Orange Bourgoin'
'Pink Ping Pong'
'Red Pear'
'Sungold'
'Tigerella'
'Yellow Cocktail'

Outside (cordon)
'Brandywine'
'Britain's Breakfast'
'King Umberto'
'Pruden's Purple'
'Ruffled Yellow'
'San Marzano'
'Yellow Perfection'

Outside (bush)
'Costoluto Fiorentino'
'Marmande'
'Pendulina'
'Phyra'
'Principe Borghese'
'Red Peach'
'Roma'
'Tiny Tim'
'Tumbler'
'Wonder Light'

FLAMME

This French cordon-type tomato is an excellent cropper. The spherical fruits, about the size of golf balls, are a beautiful apricot-orange colour and look extremely pretty when sliced. The flesh is juicy, with an intense fruity flavour, making this an excellent choice for salads and salsas. 'Flamme' makes a good pasta sauce and can also be dried successfully.

'Flamme'

HARBINGER

This cordon-type tomato was first bred around the beginning of the 20th century. It can be grown outdoors or under glass. It is indeed a harbinger of summer, fruiting early and producing medium-size tomatoes with thin, smooth skins. They have a balanced, old-fashioned tomato flavour. The fruits ripen rapidly, both on the plant and after picking. They are good varieties for salads and for garnishes.

'Harbinger'

PINK PING PONG

A robust variety, this ripens early and produces masses of unusual pinkish-red fruits the size of table tennis balls. The fruits are juicy, with a very good, sweet flavour, perfect for eating in the hand, or adding to salads.

'Pink Ping Pong'

PEELING

Add a professional finish to sauces and soups that are not being sieved by first removing the peel from the tomatoes.

1 Use a small, sharp knife – a paring knife is ideal – to cut out the green stalk end, then make a small cross in the skin on the base of each tomato.

2 Place the tomatoes in a heatproof bowl and cover with boiling water. Leave for 30 seconds, then drain. Cool slightly.

3 Gently pull away the loosened skin from the tomatoes.

Beefsteak tomatoes

Beefsteak tomatoes are a quite a new introduction to our gardens. They are large, and sometimes ugly tomatoes. One of their best virtues, besides their size, is their mild and juicy flavour. There are a number of cultivars of beefsteak tomato whose solid, meaty flesh is full of old-fashioned tomato flavour. The classic beefsteak (or beef) tomato is red, but other colours such as green, yellow, purple or the pale rose 'Florida Pink' are becoming increasingly popular. Most weigh between 350g/12oz and 450g/1lb, but there are also a few giant types, including the aptly named 'Goliath', which can top 1.3kg/3lb. For flavour, 'Brandywine' and 'Marmande' are consistent performers. Some specimens can grow extremely large, so that a single slice can be sufficient to fill a roll or sandwich. These tomatoes are also good for stuffing with a variety of fillings.

BRANDYWINE
The original 'Brandywine' was developed in America by Amish farmers in the latter half of the 19th century. The plants yield well and are disease-resistant, making them a popular choice with gardeners and growers alike. The vines grow quite tall, and have leaves that resemble those of potatoes. The reddish-pink fruits – up to 900g/2lb in weight – are noted for their succulent, rich flavour. The good balance of sweetness and acidity makes this tomato a top choice for salads.

COSTOLUTO FIORENTINO
An Italian beefsteak-type tomato, grown outdoors. The fruits are large, up to 10cm/4in in diameter, with irregular ribbing. They have a fleshy texture and exceptionally good flavour.

'Brandywine'

BLACK RUSSIAN
This tomato has a very deep red skin, almost chocolate. The dark flesh is very sweet and tasty. It is excellent sliced in salads.

'Black Russian'

GREEN ZEBRA

This tomato has stripes (dark green on a yellowish-green background, which strengthen with ripening) and looks very attractive. The tomatoes are about 7.5cm/3in across and weigh around 75g/3oz apiece. Cut them open to reveal emerald-green flesh with a sweet flavour and a subtle, spicy tang. Children love them, so put them into lunch boxes or serve in salads.

'Green Zebra'

MARMANDE

One of the few types of tomato that many people know by name, 'Marmande' originated in Provence. It does particularly well in Mediterranean regions but will also grow in cooler climes. They are best grown outdoors, as they need bees for pollination. Aromatic and fruity, these large spherical tomatoes are good for cooking and are frequently stuffed.

'Marmande'

MOON BEAM

Unlike many beefsteaks, which tend to be squat and indented, the smaller, smooth, glossy orange fruits of this early-ripening tomato are almost spherical. Thick slices taste superb in sandwiches and hamburgers, and the tomatoes can also be used to make a very tasty tomato jam or chutney.

PRUDEN'S PURPLE

Large and meaty, with few seeds, this recently rediscovered heirloom tomato resembles 'Brandywine', but it ripens earlier on in the season. The dark-red to purple fruits are large and globular, with deep pleats, and can weigh anything from 225g/ 8oz to 450g/1lb. They look and taste good. Try them in salads, or stuff them with fish or shellfish for a special Mediterranean-style treat.

RUFFLED YELLOW

The name refers to the appearance of these large tomatoes, the skin of which looks as though it has been tweaked into accordion pleats. There are several cultivars of ruffled tomatoes, and they come in red and yellow. The hollow seed cavity makes them perfect for stuffing with rice or vegetables, and they can also be hollowed out and used as an attractive and unusual container for serving a salad.

'Moon Beam'

'Pruden's Purple'

'Ruffled Yellow'

Cherry tomatoes

These small tomatoes are much more like the species tomatoes from which our modern ones are derived. They have become very popular not only because of their diminutive size, but also because of their strong, sweet flavour, which sets them aside from other forms of tomato.

CHADWICK

This bright red cherry tomato is named in honour of Alan Chadwick, who developed the biointensive method of gardening. The vigorous, disease-resistant plants bear well. 'Chadwick' tomatoes measure about 2.5cm/1in in diameter, and grow in clusters of five or six. They have a tangy flavour and taste good raw in salads or cooked in soups and sauces.

tendency to split, but the flesh is meaty, with a sweet yet tangy flavour that connoisseurs claim is what tomatoes used to taste like in the days before they were bred to meet commercial rather than culinary criteria.

PENDULINA

This is a prolific, tumbling variety, often grown in hanging baskets or tubs. The fruits are bite-size, and have a distinctive pointed tip. They may be yellow, orange or red, and have sweet, juicy flesh.

'Pendulina'

'Phyra'

PHYRA

Perfect for growing outside in hanging baskets, containers and window boxes, this bush tomato variety, which is only 30cm/12in high, produces cascades of very small fruits in various colours. Children love them for their decorative appearance and sweet flavour. They also look very attractive as a garnish, especially when left on the vine with a few leaves.

'Gardener's Delight'

'Chadwick'

GARDENER'S DELIGHT

One of the older varieties of British tomato, this is perennially popular. It is easy to grow, both outdoors and in the greenhouse, and yields a heavy crop. Long trusses bear clusters of dark red fruits, no more than 4cm/1½in in diameter. This cultivar has a slight

ROSADEL

This is one of a series (the Del series) of tomatoes bred by Lewis Darby, formerly in charge of tomato breeding at the Glasshouse Crops Research Institute in Britain. All are based on the popular 'Gardener's Delight', but are less prone to splitting. 'Rosadel' is a dainty blush-pink cordon-type cherry tomato with a wonderful flavour. It fruits quite early in the season.

'Rosadel'

'Supersweet 100'

TUMBLER

This tomato was one of the first trailing varieties specially developed for growing in containers and hanging baskets. The small red fruits make a wonderfully attractive, sprawling cascade. The bush or determinate variety is very easy to grow and produces prolific crops of bite-size bright red tomatoes over a long season. They need careful and frequent watering. They are great for picking straight of the stem and popping into your mouth. It is very useful in the kitchen for salads and for adding to snacks and lunchboxes.

'Tumbler'

SUPERSWEET 100

A hybrid version of 'Gardener's Delight', this salad tomato is usually grown in greenhouses. It is a vigorous tall, cordon variety and each truss produces up to 100 bright red cherry tomatoes, each about 2cm/¾in in diameter. The flavour is sweet, rich and well balanced. It is claimed that the 'Supersweet 100' tomato is higher in vitamin C than any other variety.

TINY TIM

Only about 2cm/¾in across, these tasty red dwarf tomatoes grow on decorative bush-type plants, which look good in tubs and hanging baskets. They are perfect for salads and as snacks.

'Tiny Tim'

FREEZING

Whole, fresh tomatoes do not freeze well, as they tend to go mushy once thawed. However, if you have a glut of tomatoes, they freeze well once they have been boiled for 5 minutes and puréed in a food processor. Allow to cool and then freeze.

Plum and pear tomatoes

These quite large, juicy and attractively shaped tomatoes have always been popular in the hotter Mediterranean climates, where they are particularly used in cooking. Increasingly, there are varieties that are more suitable for cultivation in the cooler regions.

'Andine Cornue'

ANDINE CORNUE
Also known as 'Peruvian Horn', this variety was recently introduced to Europe by a collector who brought it back from the Andes. The fruits are large and look like poblano chillies or sweet (bell) peppers with pointed ends.

BRITAIN'S BREAKFAST
Thick-skinned, with a superb flavour, this tomato is shaped like a lemon and is about the size of a hen's egg. It has a striking growth pattern, with large spreading trusses, each capable of producing more than 60 fruits. 'Britain's Breakfast' has a sweet taste and is good raw or cooked.

KING UMBERTO
Named in honour of Italy's King Umberto, this is a very old medium–early variety. It was popular in North America in the early part of the 20th century. After the 1920s it became somewhat less fashionable, but as an heirloom or heritage variety it is now making a comeback. The bright scarlet, 50g/2oz fruits can be prune- or pear-shaped and are juicy and sweet.

'King Umberto'

'Britain's Breakfast'

PRINCIPE BORGHESE
Although mainly used as a paste tomato, this aromatic Italian bush variety tastes good raw, and can also be dried very successfully. The ovoid, medium-size fruits (about 50g/2oz) are carried on large trusses and are very sugary. When grown it is in cooler climates, the flavour is very refreshing, slightly more acidic and not too sweet.

'Principe Borghese'

RED PEAR

Full of flavour, whether freshly picked or lightly cooked, this variety is particularly popular in the United States. The small fruits, which weigh around 25g/1oz each, look like party light bulbs, and grow on strong, tall vines. They are well named, being decidedly pear-shaped. There is also a yellow variety, 'Yellow Pear', which is equally popular but does not have quite such a rich taste. When sliced in half lengthways, these look pretty on a platter, especially when interleaved with basil and drizzled with olive oil.

'Red Pear'

'Roma'

SAN MARZANO

This tomato is similar to the 'Roma' variety, but the fruits are larger and more elongated in shape, and have a more intense flavour. It is an excellent all-rounder, suitable for eating fresh from the vine, but it is also ideal for sun-drying or bottling. Of Italian origin, it has sometimes been described as the original Italian tomato for sauces and pastes.

ROMA

A popular Italian plum tomato, this is a medium-to-late producing bush variety with large leaves. The scarlet fruits weigh around 50g/2oz each, and plants bear large crops. If allowed to ripen on the bush, these tomatoes have a very good flavour. They have firm, thick flesh and very few seeds, so are very good cookers and are also often used for bottling.

'San Marzano'

SEEDING

Using just the flesh of the tomato gives a meatier texture to a dish. Here are two quick methods.

1 Halve the tomatoes. Squeeze out the seeds or scoop them out with a teaspoon.

2 Cut the tomatoes into quarters. Slide a sharp knife along the inner flesh, scooping out all the seeds.

'Sun Belle'

SUN BELLE

This small yellow tomato is shaped like a plum. It is noted for its exceptional flavour, and is high in both acid and sugar. A heavy cropper, it can be grown in cold or heated greenhouses. Enjoy it fresh in salads or salsas.

Orange, yellow and green tomatoes

To gardeners of the past tomatoes were red. In recent years the search for novelty has meant that seed merchants have introduced yellow, orange and even green tomatoes. In fact they are more than just a novelty, as many of them turned out to be flavoursome and disease-resistant.

'Golden Sunrise'

GOLDEN SUNRISE

This cordon type is a heavy, reliable cropper, producing masses of medium-size round fruit. As the name suggests, they are sunshine yellow in colour. The flavour is sweet and fruity, with a slight suggestion of citrus. Slices look very pretty in a two-colour salad, and these tomatoes make an excellent garnish. Try them diced, with a light vinaigrette and a dusting of chopped mint.

JUBILEE

An American variety of tomato that requires staking, this yields medium to large globe-shaped fruits that are a rich golden-yellow or orange colour. The flavour is mild and low in acidity. Alternate slices of 'Jubilee' and 'Alicante' look pretty on a tart, or in a salad. Alternatively you can make the most of their colour by combining them with shellfish and pasta. Seed might be difficult to track down outside the United States.

MINI ORANGE

Popular some years ago but now less frequently grown, this is a bush variety that produces masses of small (2.5–4cm/1–1½in) round fruits. It is notable for its brilliant orange colour.

MIRABELLE

The small, slightly ovoid, yellow fruits have a rich, sweet flavour, similar to that of 'Gardener's Delight'. Plants of medium height produce long, heavily laden trusses. 'Mirabelle' tomatoes make a pretty garnish and are good in salsas and salads.

'Mini Orange'

'Mirabelle'

'Jubilee'

ORANGE BOURGOIN

About the same size as apricots, and almost the same colour, these juicy tomatoes have a superb flavour. Fruity, mild and sweet, they are perfect for nibbling, and taste delicious in salads. They can also look very striking, for example, when combined in a salad with orange (bell) peppers, segments of orange, and dark green leaves such as rocket (arugula) or watercress.

'Orange Bourgoin'

RED PEACH

The deep orange-rose colour of this early-ripening bush tomato, together with a fine fuzz or bloom on the skin, gives it an appearance reminiscent of a peach. The soft flesh has a mild, sweet flavour. There is also a yellow variety, which ripens to a pale, whitish-creamy colour, and whose flavour is more intense.

'Red Peach'

YELLOW PERFECTION

This a wonderful, bright yellow, award-winning cordon tomato that is excellent for salads, especially where the colour contrast is needed. It is one of the earliest of the outdoor cordon yellow varieties of tomato to produce fruit. As well as being tasty, it is also a very heavy-cropping variety.

'Yellow Perfection'

FLAME-SKINNING

If you have a gas cooker (stove), this is the simplest and quickest method for skinning a small number of tomatoes.

1 Skewer one tomato at a time on a metal fork or skewer and hold in a gas flame for 1–2 minutes, turning the tomato until the skin splits and starts to wrinkle.

2 Use a cloth to protect your hands and remove the tomato from the fork or skewer. Leave the tomatoes on a chopping board until cool enough to handle. Using your fingers or a knife, slip off and discard the skins.

ABOVE Tomatoes combine well with fresh herbs such as basil and parsley.

TIGERELLA

The name gives it away. This is a striped tomato (also known as 'Mr Stripy'), and typically has greenish-yellow or orange broken stripes on a dark red background, which is most noticeable when ripe. The small, round fruits are 4–5cm/1½–2in in diameter. A very early cordon-type, 'Tigerella' can be grown outdoors or under glass. It has a tangy, almost tart flavour, and makes a good addition to salads.

'Tigerella'

YELLOW BUTTERFLY

As pretty as its name suggests, this is a cordon-type tomato, producing slightly pear-shaped cherry tomatoes, weighing about 25g/1oz each, with a very sweet taste. It is an exceptionally heavy cropper, and grows best under glass. It makes an excellent cocktail snack if filled with soft cheese and chives, or, if you are feeling adventurous, it makes a surprisingly good dessert stewed with apples and sugar and made into a pie.

YELLOW COCKTAIL

Chefs love this bright yellow, pear-shaped, miniature tomato, which has a good taste and makes a wonderful garnish. Fruits grown indoors are best, as the skin is more tender. They also look good in salads and on kebabs, especially when alternated with red cherry tomatoes, thick slices of courgette (zucchini), chunks of aubergine (eggplant) and shallots.

'Yellow Cocktail'

'Yellow Butterfly'

CONCASSING

After peeling and seeding the tomatoes, to add the final touch to the perfect sauce or soup ingredient, concass the flesh.

Using a sharp knife, cut the flesh into neat 5mm/¼in squares.

YELLOW CURRANT

These pretty little tomatoes are close to the original tomato species. They look excellent in hanging baskets, pots and tubs. The plants on which they grow are highly ornamental, and bear extremely well. The tomatoes are reddish-orange in colour and have a pleasant, sweet flavour. Whole trusses of 'Yellow Currant' look good piled up in a bowl as a table decoration. They make delicious snacks, especially if you also offer a cream-cheese dip, flavoured with fresh herbs and spring onions (scallions).

'Wonder Light'

'Yellow Currant'

sweet but quite mild. It is a perfect tomato for use in salads, but is also a colourful addition to sauces, chutneys and other preserves.

WONDER LIGHT

A prolific producer, this bush tomato always needs staking, as the branches tend to bend under the fairly heavy weight of the 7.5cm/3in long fruits, which are lemon-yellow in colour and also rather like lemons in shape. These tomatoes have a good rich flavour.

'Yellow Oxheart'

YELLOW OXHEART

Meaty and flavoursome, this is a bright yellow heart-shaped tomato, about 400–450g/14oz–1lb in weight. Like other beefsteak tomatoes, it is a cordon type, with lacy foliage. The chunky tomato has few seeds.

YELLOW PEAR

A very old variety from the 19th century. It has a yellow skin and a classic pear shape. The flavour is

Amish Paste
An American heirloom cordon-type tomato from Wisconsin. The 225g/8oz fruits are large and elongated, with a deep red colour. Firm and meaty, with few seeds and low acidity, 'Amish Paste' tomatoes are used for canning and for sauces.

Black Krym
For a dramatic effect, there are few tomatoes to equal this one. The skin is of such a deep tone of red that it often appears to be black, with a hint of dark green on the heavy shoulders. It comes from the Black Sea port of Krymsk and is sometimes known as 'Black Russian'. The very large, slightly irregular fruits can weigh up to 350g/12oz and have maroon flesh, noted for its delicate, melting tenderness and rich, complex flavour.

Costoluto Genovese
A prolific variety from the Italian Riviera, first recorded in 1805. This scarlet, ribbed tomato loves hot climates and is grown throughout the Mediterranean. The large, attractive fruits average about 200g/7oz. They have a meaty texture and are full-flavoured with a hint of acidity. They look similar to 'Pruden's Purple', but are more deeply lobed. The ribbing ensures that they look good sliced in salads, but they also cook well and make fine pasta sauces.

Golden Amateur
A short-growing variety suitable for indoor or outside cultivation, its size making it ideal for smaller gardens. The yellow fruits are produced in large numbers.

planning and
preparation

Like so many vegetables and fruits, tomatoes
can be easily grown in the garden, and a few
plants, in containers or in the ground, will
take up little space but provide fruits
throughout summer and into autumn.
As long as you take a little trouble to
improve the quality of your soil and
to make sure that you provide good
growing conditions, you will be
rewarded with a delicious, plentiful crop.

Types of soil

Tomatoes can be grown on almost any type of soil, but rich, fertile, well-drained soil is the optimum with a pH range of 5.5–7. Most soils can be persuaded, with varying degrees of effort, to move towards that optimum, but soils vary greatly in different areas and some are easier to deal with than others. Tomatoes are best grown in the same site every year.

CLAY

When they work well clay soils can be excellent, because of their high fertility, but their structure is the despair of most gardeners.

WORKING IN ORGANIC MATTER

1 Soil that has been dug in the autumn can have more organic matter worked into the top layer in the spring. Spread the organic matter over the surface.

2 Lightly work the organic material into the top layer of soil with a fork. There is no need for full-scale digging.

Clay is heavy, and the particles cling together, making the soil sticky. Clay soil compacts easily, forming a solid lump that roots find hard to penetrate and that is difficult to dig. Try not to walk on clay soils when they are wet. This tendency to become compacted and sticky means that clay soils are slow to drain, but, once drained, they set like concrete, becoming a hard mass. They also tend to be cold and slow to warm up, making them unsuitable for early crops, but slow to cool down in autumn.

SANDY SOILS

Soils that are made up of sand and silts are quite different to clay soils. Sandy soils have few of the sticky clay particles but are made up of individual grains that allow the water to pass through quickly. This quick passage of water through the soil tends to leach (wash) out nutrients, so the soils are often poor. However, they also tend to be much warmer in winter and are quicker to warm up in spring, thus making it easier to get early crops.

Silts contain particles that are rather more clay-like in structure allowing them to hold slightly more moisture and more nutrients than sandy soils. Both sandy and clay soil are easy to improve and are not difficult to work. Sand does not compact like clay does (although it is still not good practice to walk on beds), but silty soils are more susceptible to the impact of feet

WORKING ON WET SOIL

It is best to avoid working on wet soil, but sometimes it is necessary. To ensure that the soil is not compacted and its structure destroyed, it is advisable to work from a plank of wood.

and wheelbarrows. Adding organic material adds bulk and can temper their insatiable thirst.

LOAMS

The soil of most gardeners' dreams is loam. This is a combination of clay and sandy soils, with the best elements of both. They tend to be free-draining, but at the same time moisture-retentive. This description – free-draining and moisture-retentive – is often used of soils and potting mixes and it may seem a contradiction. It means that the soil is sufficiently free-draining to allow excess moisture to drain away, but enough moisture is retained for the plant's needs without it standing in stagnant water. Such soils are easy to work and are excellent for tomatoes, and they warm up well in spring and are thus good for early crops.

1 Collect the soil sample 5–8cm/2–3in below the surface. Take a number of samples, and test each one separately.

2 With this kit, mix one part soil with five parts water. Shake well in a jar, then allow the water to settle.

3 Draw off some of the settled liquid from the top few centimetres (about an inch) for your test.

4 Carefully transfer the solution to the test chamber in the plastic container, using the pipette.

5 Select a colour-coded capsule (one for each nutrient). Put the powder in the chamber, replace the cap and shake.

6 After a few minutes, compare the colour of the liquid with the shade panel of the container.

ACID AND ALKALINE SOILS

Another way of classifying soils is by their acidity or alkalinity. Those that are based on peat (peat moss) are acid; those that include chalk or limestone are alkaline. Gardeners use a scale of pH levels to indicate the degree of acidity or alkalinity. Very acid is 1, neutral is 7 and very alkaline is 14, although soils rarely have values at the extremes of the scale. Although they can be grown on a wide range of soils, tomatoes are usually grown in soils with a pH of 5.5–7, with the optimum conditions being around 6.5. So,

the best pH for growing tomatoes is slightly on the acid side of neutral. A test with a soil-kit will show the rating in your own garden. It is easy to make an acid soil more alkaline, but adjusting alkaline soils is more difficult.

IMPROVING HEAVY SOIL

In very wet sites you may need to dig drainage channels, but in many gardens, simply improving the soil will enable water to drain away. One way to achieve this is to add organic material. The fibrous material contained within the

organic matter helps to break up the clay particles, allowing water to pass through. This eventually breaks down and so it should be added every time the soil is dug.

The other method is to add gravel or grit to the soil. The best material for this is generally known as horticultural grit – that is, sharp grit up to about 5mm/¼in in diameter. Flint grit that has been crushed is the best type because the angular faces allow water to drain away better than the rounded surfaces of the uncrushed grits, such as peabeach.

Soil improvement

Another way of improving the quality of the soil is to adjust the pH level. Tomatoes will grow well in a wide range of fairly fertile, well-drained soils provided that the soil's pH is between 5.5 and 7.

TESTING pH

Soil-testing kits are widely available from garden centres and many general stores. They are cheap and easy to use. Take samples from various places in the garden because previous gardeners might have treated the soil, which will influence the reading. Follow the directions on the box about mixing the soil samples with distilled water and check the resulting solution against the chart supplied.

Although soil meters are available – simply insert the end of the meter in the ground and see how the needle on the gauge moves – these are not reliable indicators of pH levels and should be used with caution.

CHANGING pH LEVELS

If the soil is too acid, the pH can be adjusted somewhat by adding lime to the soil. Three types of lime can be used for reducing soil acidity. Ordinary lime (calcium carbonate) is the easiest and safest to use. Quicklime (calcium oxide) is easy to apply and is the strongest and most caustic, but it may cause damage. Slaked lime (calcium hydroxide) is quicklime with water added; it is not as strong as quicklime and is much safer for the gardener to use.

Always wear gloves when you are applying lime and follow the quantities recommended by the manufacturer on the packet. Do not add lime at the same time as manure, because this will release ammonia, which can damage the plants. Spread the lime over the soil at the rate prescribed on the packet and rake it in. Do not sow or plant in the ground for at least a month. Do not over-lime.

It is not as easy to reduce the alkalinity of soil. Peat (peat moss) used to be recommended for this purpose, but not only is collecting peat environmentally unsound, it breaks down very quickly and needs to be constantly replaced. Most organic manures are slightly acid and help to bring down the

pH VALUES	
1.0	extremely acid
4.0	maximum acidity tolerated by most plants
5.5	maximum acidity for reasonable tomatoes
6.0	maximum acidity for good tomatoes
6.5	optimum for the best tomatoes
7.0	neutral, maximum alkalinity for good tomatoes
7.5	maximum alkalinity for reasonable vegetables
8.0	maximum tolerated by most plants
14.0	extremely alkaline

levels. Leaf mould, especially that from pine trees, is also acid. Spent mushroom compost contains lime and is useful for reducing acidity, but it should not be used on chalky (alkaline) soils.

LEFT The acidity of the soil can be reduced by adding lime some weeks before planting and working it in with a rake. Check the soil with a soil-testing kit to see how much lime is required.

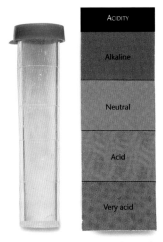

ABOVE You can test the pH of the soil by using one of a range of soil testers.

Soil structure

Perhaps the most important task in any garden is to improve and maintain the quality of the soil. Good quality soil should be the aim of any gardener who wants to grow vegetables or fruit. To ignore the soil is to ignore one of the garden's most important assets.

ORGANIC MATERIAL

The key to improving the soil in your garden is organic material. This is an all-embracing term that covers any vegetable matter that has been broken down into an odourless, fibrous compost. It includes such things as rotted garden waste, kitchen vegetable waste, farmyard manures (which are plant materials that have passed through animals) and other plant waste material.

It is important that any such material should be well rotted. If it is still in the process of breaking down, it will need nitrogen to complete the process and will extract it from the soil. This, of course, is the reverse of what the gardener wants – the gardener's aim is, in fact, to add nitrogen to the soil. If you are unsure, a good indicator that the material has broken down sufficiently is that it becomes odourless. Even horse manure is free from odour once it has rotted down, and manuring a garden should not be the smelly task it is often imagined to be.

Some substances contain undesirable chemicals, but these will be removed if the material is stacked and allowed to weather. Bark and other shredded woody materials may contain resins, for example, while animal and bird manures may contain ammonia from urea. These chemicals will eventually evaporate or be converted by weathering.

ABOVE The fertility of the soil is much improved by the addition of organic material, but a quick boost can also be achieved by adding an organic fertilizer, spreading it over the surface and then raking it in.

DIGGING IN

The best way to apply organic material to the vegetable garden is to dig it in. In this way it becomes incorporated into the soil. If possible, double dig the bed, adding material all the way to the bottom of both spits. This will help to improve the structure and supply nutrients where they are needed.

IMPROVING SOIL STRUCTURE

1 One of the best ways to improve the structure of the soil is to add as much organic material as you can, preferably when the soil is dug. For heavy soils, this is best done in the autumn.

2 If the soil has already been dug, well-rotted organic material can be worked into the surface of the soil with a fork. The worms will complete the task of working it into the soil.

Compost

This is a valuable material for any garden, but it is especially useful in the vegetable garden. It is free, apart from any capital required to install compost bins, and these should last many years, so the overall cost should be negligible. A little effort is required, but this is a small price to pay for the resulting gold dust.

THE PRINCIPLE

The idea behind compost-making is to emulate the process by which a plant takes nutrients from the soil, dies and then rots, putting the nutrients back into the ground. In the garden, waste plant material is collected, piled in a heap and allowed to rot down before being returned to the soil as crumbly, sweet-smelling, fibrous material.

Because it is kept in a heap the rotting material generates heat, which encourages it to break down even more quickly. The heat also helps to kill pests and diseases as well as any weed seed contained in the compost. If the rotting material is to break down properly, a certain amount of moisture is needed, as well as air. The compost should be moist, but not wet or waterlogged. If there is insufficient air, the heap will go slimy and smell bad. The process should take up to about three months.

THE COMPOST BIN

Gardeners always seem to generate more garden waste than they ever thought possible and never to have enough compost space, so when you are planning your bins, make sure you have enough. The ideal is to have three: one to hold new waste, one that is in the process of breaking down, and the third that is ready for use.

Bins are traditionally made from wood (often scrap wood), and since these can be hand-made to fit your space and the amount of material available, this is still the best option. Sheet materials, such as corrugated iron, can also be used. Most ready-made bins are made of plastic, and although these work well, they may be rather small for a busy garden.

A bin should contain at least a cubic metre/35 cubic feet of compost for it to heat up. If you have a large garden, a bin twice

ABOVE A range of organic materials can be used, but avoid cooked kitchen waste or any weeds that have seed in them. *Clockwise from top left:* kitchen waste, weeds, shreddings and grass clippings.

this size would be even more efficient. A simple bin can be made by nailing together four wooden pallets to form a box. If the front of the container is made so that the slats are slotted in to form the wall, they can be removed as the bin is emptied, making the job of removing the compost easier.

LEFT Good compost is dark brown, crumbly and has a sweet, earthy smell, not a rotting one.

RIGHT Green manure helps to improve both the structure and fertility of the soil. Sow it when the ground is not being used for anything else and then dig it in before it flowers and seeds.

MATERIALS

Most garden plant waste can be used for composting, but do not include diseased material, perennial weed roots or seeding weeds. Woody material, such as hedge clippings, can be used, but shred it first. Kitchen vegetable waste, such as peelings and cores, can be used, but avoid cooked vegetables. Do not include animal products, which will attract rats and other vermin. You could have a separate bin for seeding weeds, as the compost can be used for permanent plantings such as trees. Compost used for this purpose will never come to the surface, and any seeds will be prevented from germinating.

TECHNIQUE

Placing twiggy material in the bottom of the bin will help to keep the contents aerated. Put in the material as it becomes available but avoid building up deep layers of any one material, especially grass cuttings. Mix them up well.

To help keep the heap warm, cover it with an old carpet or a sheet of polythene (plastic). This also prevents excess water from chilling the contents as well as swamping all the air spaces. The lid should be kept on until the compost is ready to be used.

Every so often, add a layer of farmyard manure if you can get it because it will provide extra nitrogen to speed up the process of decomposition. Failing this, you can buy special compost accelerators. It is not essential to add manure or an accelerator, however – it just means waiting a few weeks longer for your compost.

Air is important, and this usually percolates through the side of the bin, so leave a few gaps between the timbers. Old pallets are usually crudely made, with plenty of gaps anyway. The colder material around the edges takes longer to break down than in the centre of the heap, so turn the compost around every so often. This also loosens the pile and allows air through the material.

MAKING COMPOST

1 A simple compost bin, which should be about 1m/3ft square, can be made by nailing together four flat pallets with plenty of air holes between the slats.

2 Pile the waste into the compost bin, making certain that there are no thick layers of the same material. Do not put in thick layers of grass clippings.

3 Keep the compost bin covered with a mat or a sheet of polythene (sheet vinyl or plastic). This will keep in the heat and prevent the compost getting too wet.

4 Turn the contents of the bin with a fork, partly to let in air and partly to move the outside material, which is slow to rot, to the centre.

5 If you like, add a layer of soil to grow courgettes (zucchini). To use the compost sooner, just keep covered with a polythene (plastic) sheet.

Soil conditioners

A range of organic conditioners is available to the gardener. Some are free – if you do not count the time taken in working and carting them. Others are relatively cheap, and some, usually those bought by the bag, can be quite expensive. However, not everyone has a stable nearby or enough space to store large quantities of material, and many gardeners will therefore need to buy it as required.

FARMYARD MANURE

A traditional material and still much used by many country gardeners, farmyard manure has the advantage of adding bulk to the soil as well as supplying valuable nutrients. The manure can come from any form of livestock, although the most commonly available is horse manure. It can be obtained from most stables, and many are so glad to get rid of it that they will supply it free if you fetch it yourself. There are often stables situated around the edge of towns, so manure is usually available to town gardeners as well as to those in the country.

Some gardeners do not like to use the manure when it is mixed with wood shavings rather than with straw, but it is worth bearing in mind that the former is often less likely to contain weed seeds, and as long as it is stacked and allowed to rot down it is excellent for adding to the soil as well as for use as a top-dressing. All manures should be stacked for at least six months before they are used. When the manure is ready, it will have lost its dungy smell and have become a dark, friable mix.

GARDEN COMPOST

All gardeners should try to recycle as much of their garden and kitchen vegetable waste as possible. In essence, this is simply following nature's pattern, where leaves and stems are formed in the spring and die back in the autumn, falling to the ground and eventually rotting and returning to the soil as nutrients. In the garden some things are removed from the cycle, notably vegetables and fruit, but as much material as possible should be recirculated. Unless diseased plants or perennial or seeding weeds have been used, well-made compost should be safe to use as a soil conditioner and as a mulch.

LEAF MOULD

This is a natural soil conditioner. It is easy to make and should not cost anything. Only use leaf mould made by yourself; never go to local woods and help yourself as this will disturb the wood's own cycle and will impoverish the soil there.

Four stakes knocked into the ground with a piece of wirenetting stretched around them will make the perfect container for making leaf mould. Simply add the leaves as they fall from the trees. It will take a couple of years for them to break down and what was a huge heap will shrink to a small layer by the time the process is complete. If you are in a hurry, it is also possible to buy accelerators which will speed up the process so that leaf mould is available within a year.

Add leaf mould to the soil or use it as a top-dressing. It is usually acid and can be used to reduce the pH of alkaline soil. Leaf mould from pine needles is particularly acid.

SOME ORGANIC MATERIALS

Well-rotted farmyard manure

Well-rotted garden compost

Fertilizers

You cannot go on taking things out of the soil without putting anything back. In nature plants return the nutrients they have taken from the soil when they die. In the garden the vegetables are removed and eaten, and the chain is broken. Compost and other organic materials help to redress the balance, but if there are not enough to do the job properly fertilizers are needed.

WHAT PLANTS REQUIRE

The main foods required by plants are nitrogen (N), phosphorus (P) and potassium (K), with smaller quantities of magnesium (Mg), calcium (Ca) and sulphur (S). They also require small amounts of trace elements, including iron (Fe) and manganese (Mn).

Each of the main nutrients tends to be used by the plant for one specific function. Nitrogen is used for promoting the rapid growth of the green parts of the plant. Phosphorus, usually in the form of phosphates, is used to encourage good root growth as well as helping with the ripening of fruits. Potassium, in the form of potash, is used to promote flowering and formation of good fruit. It is the main ingredient in tomato feed.

ORGANIC FERTILIZERS

Concentrated fertilizers are of two types: organic and inorganic. Organic fertilizers consist solely of naturally occurring materials and contain different proportions of nutrients. So bonemeal (ground-up bones), which is strong in phosphates and nitrogen, promotes growth, especially root growth. Bonemeal also has the advantage that it breaks down slowly, gradually releasing the fertilizer over a long period. (Wear gloves when you apply bonemeal.)

Other organic fertilizers include fish, blood and bone (high in nitrogen and phosphates); hoof and horn (nitrogen); and seaweed meal (nitrogen and potash). Because they are derived from natural products without any modification, they are used by organic growers.

INORGANIC FERTILIZERS

These are fertilizers that have been made artificially, although they are frequently derived from natural rocks and minerals and the process may just involve crushing. They are concentrated and are usually soluble in water. This means that they are instantly available for the plant. They do, however, tend to wash out of the soil quickly and need to be replaced.

Some are general fertilizers, and might contain equal proportions of nitrogen, phosphorus and potassium. Others are specific: superphosphate, for example, is entirely used for supplying phosphorus, while potassium sulphate is added when potassium is required.

SLOW-RELEASE FERTILIZERS

A new trend is to coat the fertilizers so that they are released slowly into the soil. These are expensive in the short term, but because they do not leach away and do not need to be replaced as frequently, they are more economic in the longer term. They are useful for container planting, where constant watering is necessary which dissolves and washes away normal fertilizer.

ORGANIC FERTILIZERS

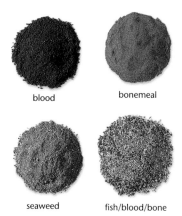

blood   bonemeal

seaweed   fish/blood/bone

INORGANIC FERTILIZERS

Growmore (not   sulphate of
available in USA)   ammonia

potash   superphosphate

Digging and breaking down

One of the main garden activities, digging breaks up the soil, allowing the ingress of water and air, which are both important for plant growth. It also allows organic material to be incorporated deep down in the soil, right where the roots need it.

All weeds and their roots can be removed during digging, which also brings pests to the surface so that they can be removed and destroyed. It also allows the gardener to keep an eye on the condition of the soil. Some organic gardeners now advocate a no-dig method of growing tomatoes, fruits and vegetables.

SINGLE DIGGING

The most frequently carried out method is single digging, of which there are two ways, one informal and the other formal.

In the informal method the ground is usually already quite loose, and the gardener simply forks it over, turning it over and replacing it in the same position,

SINGLE DIGGING

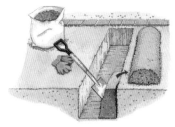

1 Start by digging a trench across the plot, putting the soil from the first trench to one side to be used later in the final trench.

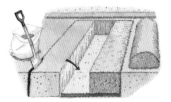

3 Repeat this process of adding manure to each trench and filling in with earth from the next, breaking up the soil as you go and keeping the surface even.

hardly using any trench at all. This process is more frequently carried out on light or sandy soils.

Formal single digging is necessary on heavier soils, and it is carried out when there is organic material to be incorporated. First, a trench is dug across the width of the plot, and the earth taken from this is carried, usually in a wheelbarrow, to the other end of the bed. Compost or manure is put into the bottom of the trench and

LEFT After a winter exposed to the weather, most soils will be easy to break down into a fine tilth using a rake.

2 Put a layer of manure in the bottom of the trench. Dig out the next trench and cover the manure with earth taken from the second trench.

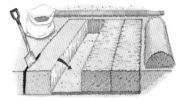

4 Continue down the length of the plot until you reach the final trench. This should be filled in with the earth taken from the first trench.

then another trench is dug. This time, the earth removed from the trench is put into the first trench to cover the organic material. This procedure is repeated down the length of the plot. When the final trench has been dug and organic material placed in it, it is refilled with the soil from the first trench.

Further refinements can be applied. For example, the first trench can be dug so that it is two trenches wide. Organic material is put in the bottom as usual, and then the next trench is dug but the soil is spread over the bottom of the first, double-width trench, only half-filling it.

This is then covered with another layer of organic material and then the third trench dug, filling up the first. This sequence is then repeated, beginning with another double-width trench. This method makes for a better distribution of the organic material through the soil.

BREAKING UP SUBSOIL

Use the double digging method to break up the subsoil. This is useful to do on new plots of ground as well as when deep beds are being prepared. Dig the trench as before, taking the earth to the end of the plot. Then dig the soil in the bottom of the trench to the depth of a fork, adding organic material.

Add more organic material on top and then dig the next trench, placing the soil into the first. Repeat until the end of the plot is reached. Do not bring any subsoil to the top. A method requiring more energy but giving better results is to dig out the first trench and then dig another below it, keeping the two soils separate. Dig out the top spit of the next trench and also put this to one side. Add organic material to the first double trench and dig the bottom spit of the second trench into it. Add more compost, then take the top spit of the third trench and place this on top of the new soil in the bottom of the first trench. Work down the plot and then fill in the remaining trenches.

DOUBLE DIGGING

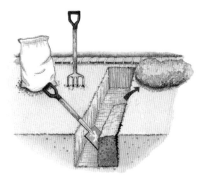

1 Dig a wide trench, placing the soil to one side to be used later when filling in the final trench.

2 Break up the soil at the bottom of the trench, adding manure to the soil as you proceed.

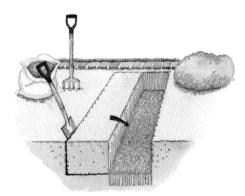

3 Dig the next trench, turning the soil over on top of the broken soil in the first trench.

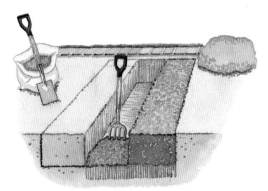

4 Continue down the plot, ensuring that subsoil from the lower trench is not mixed with topsoil of the upper.

Greenhouses

The goal of most gardeners is to have a greenhouse, for it extends the possibilities of the garden adn growing different tomato varieties tremendously. Such a structure can be used for propagation, for growing tender or winter crops and for overwintering plants that cannot be safely left outside. There is a fourth, often unspoken, use and that is to keep the gardener dry and warm in winter.

CHOOSING A GREENHOUSE

As with any equipment, the first thing to consider is your reason for making the purchase. Why do you want a greenhouse? Are you only going to grow tomatoes in it? This is an important stage, because answering these questions will help to determine the size. Cost and the available space will also obviously influence the size, but if possible, make use the prime consideration. Most gardeners, slightly tongue in cheek, will tell you to work out the size and then double it. Many, if not most, gardeners wish that they had bought a larger greenhouse than the one they did. So buy larger rather than smaller if you possibly can.

MATERIAL

These days the choice is mainly between wood and aluminium, although it is still possible to find old iron-frame greenhouses, and some more expensive ones are a combination of materials, such as brick and wood. For most gardeners the choice is simply an aluminium frame, because it is the cheapest style available, but there are other factors to take into consideration. For example, wooden greenhouses are far more attractive than aluminium ones, and they are slightly warmer in winter. However, although they usually fit sympathetically into the garden, they are more expensive and the upkeep is more time-consuming. It is possible to make your own, working to your own design and dimensions to fit your needs.

Aluminium greenhouses are easy to maintain, and cheap. The cheaper ones may, however, be rather flimsy, and in exposed positions the sides may flex and the glass fall out! They normally come in standard sizes, but because they are modular, there is a choice of the number of windows and their position. Some companies will build to your specifications, but this is obviously a more expensive option. It is now possible to buy aluminium greenhouses where the frame is painted, which partially disguises the aluminium.

Glass can now be replaced with plastic. Most gardeners prefer the glass, but if there are children around it is often more sensible to go for plastic on safety grounds.

DIGGING IN

The old-fashioned idea of sinking the greenhouse into the ground is a good one as long as you can overcome any drainage problems. Steps lead down to the door, and on to a central aisle, dug out of the soil. The side benches are laid on the natural soil level and the roof

LEFT This standard straight-sided greenhouse is made of aluminium, but it has been painted green, rather than being left silver, so that it blends in better with the colours of the garden.

springs from a low wall on the ground. The advantage of this system, apart from the fact that it is fairly cheap, is that the soil acts as a vast storage heater. Gardeners using such a greenhouse find that as long as they provide some form of insulation, no heat is required to overwinter tender plants. Typically, a wooden framework would have been used for the roof, but aluminium would do just as well.

SHAPE

The shape of the greenhouse is up to personal choice. Traditional styles have vertical sides, but some new ones have sloping sides, which allow in more light – especially useful during winter when the sun is low or if you have trays of seedlings on the floor.

Octagonal greenhouses are suitable for small sites, and many people find them more decorative than the traditional shapes. Because they are almost round, the "aisle" is just a central standing area, thus saving a lot of wasted space. However, the amount of useful space is still quite small.

Lean-to greenhouses can be built against walls, which not only saves space but also makes use of the warmth that is usually found in walls, especially house walls. These are much cheaper than a full greenhouse, but the amount of useful space within them is limited because the light does not come from all directions and plants can suffer. Painting the wall white helps because more light is reflected back on to the plants.

VENTILATION

When you buy a greenhouse, make sure that it has as many opening windows as you can afford, because the free passage of air through the structure is important. Stagnant air in a greenhouse is a killer, as all kinds of fungal diseases are likely to develop very quickly. Openings can either be covered with conventional windows or with louvres. If you are away during daylight hours in summer, the time

ABOVE A greenhouse with a steeply pitched roof that not only looks different from conventional greenhouses, but has the added advantage that the steep sides absorb the low winter sun more easily.

when windows need to be opened on hot days, automatic openers can be used. The mechanism opens the windows as soon as a specified pre-set temperature is reached. Having a door at each end helps on larger houses. In winter,

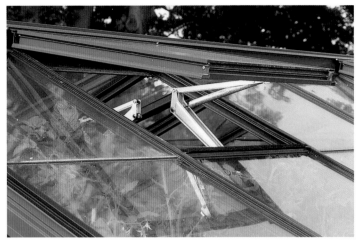

LEFT Do not let greenhouses overheat. Opening windows at the right time is not always possible if you are not at home during the hottest part of the day, but automatic window-openers will do the job.

have only a few plants that need protecting, it is cheaper to close off one end of the greenhouse with plastic sheeting and heat just this area. If the number of plants is small enough, a heated propagator or a cloche over a heated bench may be sufficient.

SHADING

Greenhouses need to be as light as possible, especially during the winter, but at the same time bright sunshine should be kept out as this will raise the temperature too much. It is possible to buy shade netting, which can be draped over the outside or clipped to the inside of the glass. This is easy to remove in overcast periods. An opaque wash applied to the glass reduces

windows should be left open as much as possible without losing too much heat, and, when it is necessary to close them, use a fan to keep the air circulating.

HEATING

There are various ways of heating a greenhouse, but one of the most versatile is with electricity. Although the cost per unit of heat may be greater, the control of its output through the use of thermostats is such that no heat (or money) is wasted, because the appliance comes on only when the temperature drops below a certain point. Thermostatically controlled gas heaters are also now becoming available. Paraffin heaters are cheap, but they need to be regularly filled and maintained and

they produce large amounts of water vapour, which encourages disease unless the greenhouse is well ventilated.

Heating bills can be reduced by insulating the greenhouse. Double glazing is the ultimate but is expensive. A cheaper alternative is to line the house with sheets of clear plastic, preferably the type that contains air bubbles. If you

RIGHT Insulating the greenhouse is vital during the cold winter months, helping to keep heating costs down as well as preventing any fluctuations in temperature. Plastic bubble insulation is efficient.

the effect of the sun considerably, but it is time-consuming to keep removing it during dull weather, so it is usually left in place from early summer to mid-autumn. There is one form of wash that becomes transparent when it rains, thus letting in more light.

FITTINGS

The full height of the greenhouse is needed for tomatoes, which can be grown in growing bags on the floor. Benching or staging is a useful addition, at least down one side, and can be made of wood or longer-lasting aluminium.

If the staging has raised sides it can be filled with sand. This is very useful for sinking pots in to help keep them warm and moist. Heating cables can also be used to keep the bench warm, and building a plastic or glass cabinet or lid on top will turn it into an effective propagating bench.

POLYTUNNELS

Polythene (plastic) tunnels are a cheap alternative to greenhouses. They are ideal for growing winter and early spring vegetables and for housing and propagating plants until they are ready to plant out. They are, however, rather ugly and can get very cold, and the covering will need replacing every three years or so.

MAINTENANCE

Greenhouses can become a hotbed of pests and diseases unless they are well maintained. Clear everything out at least once a year. Wash down with disinfectant or shut all the vents and light a special smoke bomb, which will fumigate the greenhouse and its fittings. Remove any diseased plants as they occur and burn them. At the end of the season clean out all the old plants as soon as they

ABOVE Netting is a good way to protect the greenhouse from strong sun during the hottest part of the year.

have finished cropping. If you have used growing bags or any other form of container system, remove the old compost, which can be used elsewhere in the garden to help condition the soil. If the soil is in beds then it should be dug out and replaced every other year.

Wash down the glass and treat the structure with preservative if it is made of wood. In autumn and early winter, check that the heating systems and propagating units work, so you can begin planting in spring.

ABOVE Electric fan heaters are efficient. When equipped with thermostats, they only come on when extra heat is required.

LEFT A maximum/minimum thermometer is ideal for keeping track of the temperature in a greenhouse, warning you to adjust the conditions before the plants suffer.

cultivating
tomatoes

Growing tomatoes is not difficult,
and even first-time growers should be able
to produce fruits from midsummer into
autumn. In the garden they need fertile,
well-drained soil and sun; in the greenhouse
they also need regular watering and feeding.
Most gardeners have their favourite cultivars,
chosen because of their taste, colour or ease of
growing, but it is a good idea to try at least a
few new varieties each season. If you are
interested in growing some of the more
unusual cultivars, a greenhouse will make it
easier to raise your own plants from seed.

Sowing under glass

Raising tomatoes from seed is not only cheaper than buying small plants, it also gives the gardener a far wider range of cultivars than will be available as plants from garden centres or nurseries. However, in most temperate regions the seeds will need to be sown under glass. Even outdoor varieties of tomato cannot normally be sown straight in the ground, since by the time the soil is warm enough for germination to take place, it is often too late for them to grow to the size necessary to produce a good crop in the summer.

CONTAINERS

Seeds can be sown in a variety of containers. Traditionally they were sown in wooden trays or flats. Some gardeners prefer to make their own, claiming that they are warmer and that they can be made deeper than the purchased ones. Plastic trays, which have generally replaced the wooden varieties, can be made of rigid plastic for repeated use or thin, flimsy plastic, to be used only once before being thrown away.

Often, only a few plants may be required, and it is rather wasteful to sow a whole or half tray. A 9cm/3½in pot is usually sufficient.

Many gardeners are using modular or cellular trays, in which one or two seeds are sown in a small cell. If both germinate, one is removed and the remaining seedling is allowed to develop without having to be pricked out. This method avoids a lot of root disturbance.

PROPAGATORS

These are glass or plastic boxes that help to keep the seed tray moist and in a warm atmosphere. The more expensive models have heating cables in them so that the temperature can be controlled. Cheaper alternatives can also be made simply by slipping the tray

ABOVE A range of pots and trays is now available that are suitable for sowing many seeds. Clockwise from top left: individual cells or modules, a half tray, plastic pots, a fibrous pot and modules.

into a plastic bag and removing it as soon as the seeds have germinated. Plastic bottles can also be cut down to fit over the top of individual pots.

HEAT

A source of heat is useful for the rapid germination of seeds. It can be provided in the form of a heated propagator, but most seeds will

BELOW Fill the pot with a good seed compost (soil mix), tap it on the bench and sow one to three seeds in each pot. Once germinated, the weaker seedlings will be removed, leaving one to grow on.

BELOW Fill the cellular block with compost (soil mix) and tap it on the table to firm it down. Sow one or two seeds in each cell. Cover with a light dusting of compost.

LEFT Watering from below avoids disturbing the newly planted seeds.

germinate in the temperature of a warm greenhouse or conservatory (porch), or even within the house.

SOWING SEED

Fill a seed tray or pot with a good quality seed or potting compost (soil mix). Gently firm down and sow the seeds thinly on the surface. Tomatoes should be sown no earlier than six to eight weeks before you intend to transplant them, otherwise they may become rootbound. Spread a thin layer of compost over the seeds so that they are just covered. Again, firm down lightly.

Water by placing the seed tray or pot in a shallow bowl of water, so that the level of the water comes halfway up the sides. Once the surface of the compost shows signs of dampness, remove the tray or pot and place it in a propagator or in a plastic bag. A traditional alternative – and one that still works well – is to place a sheet of glass over the tray.

SOWING IN CELLS

Fill the cellular block with compost and tap it on the table to firm it down. Sow one or two seeds in each cell. Cover with a light dusting of compost. Label the tray, especially if you are growing several different varieties. Water from below as before, then place in a propagator or plastic bag. Remove the weaker of the two seedlings after germination.

USING A PROPAGATOR

1 Place the seeds in a propagator. You can adjust the temperature of heated propagators like this. The ideal temperature for tomatoes is 16°C/61°F, but you may need to compromise if you are growing other plants as well.

2 This propagator is unheated and should be kept in a warm position in a greenhouse or within the house. Start opening the vents once the seeds have germinated to begin the hardening-off process.

SUBSEQUENT TREATMENT

As soon as the seeds begin to germinate, remove the lid from the propagator – or open the bag, depending on the method you are using – to let in air, and after a couple of days remove the tray altogether. If you are using a propagator, turn off the heat and open the vents over a few days and then remove the tray.

Once the seedlings are large enough to handle, prick them out into individual pots. Hold the seedlings by the seed-leaves and not by the stem or roots. Keep them warm and watered.

If you are going to plant them outside, gradually harden them off first by exposing them to outdoor conditions for a little longer each day until they can be safely left out overnight. They are then ready to plant out.

Greenhouse tomatoes

Glasshouses allow gardeners to maintain a constant environment for the tomato plants and to provide shelter from inclement weather as well as consistent humidity, air, water, nutrients and light. This extends the length of the growing season and increases the yield of the plants.

GROWING FROM SEED

When growing under glass, sow the seed in mid-spring in a gentle heat or an unheated greenhouse. An earlier start can be made in a heated greenhouse to obtain earlier crops. As soon as they are big enough to handle, prick out the seedlings into individual pots. When the tomato plants are large enough, transfer them to growing bags, pots or a greenhouse border. The soil will need changing, preferably every year, if tomatoes are planted directly into a border.

Arrange a form of support, such as strings or canes, for the tomatoes to be tied to as they grow. Remove any sideshoots as they appear. Keep well watered and feed every ten days with a high-potash liquid fertilizer once the fruits have begun to swell. Pinch out the top of the plant when it reaches the glass.

CULTIVATION INDOORS

Sowing time: early to mid-spring
Sowing inside: in modules or pots
Planting time: mid- to late spring
Planting and sowing distance: 45cm/18in
Harvesting: summer onwards

PLANTING TOMATOES

Traditionally, greenhouse tomatoes were always grown in the greenhouse border. More recently, growing bags and other types of containers have been in favour. Other methods are used commercially, but three practical and easy methods are suitable for gardeners with small greenhouses: beds, growing bags and ring culture. All three systems have merits and drawbacks, but how well you look after your tomatoes while they are growing can be as important as the system itself.

If planting directly into greenhouse beds, it advisable to replace the soil at least every other year. Growing bags are the easiest method of growing tomatoes in a greenhouse. Directions are usually given on the bag but it is simplicity itself, with the tomatoes planted through holes made in the bag.

Ring culture is worth considering once the border ceases to be productive. Make a trench in the border and line it with plastic to reduce the risk of contamination from the underlying soil. Place fine

LEFT Pots of French marigolds will deter whitefly from your tomato plants.

1 Before planting directly into the borders, dig in as much manure or garden compost as you can and rake in a garden fertilizer. Although tomatoes can be planted earlier, most amateurs find late spring is a good time as the greenhouse usually has more space once the bedding plants have been moved out.

2 Most greenhouse varieties grow tall and need support. Tall canes are a convenient method if you have just a few plants, but if you have a lot of plants the string method may be more suitable.

3 With ring culture, the water-absorbing roots grow into a moist aggregate and the feeding roots into special bottomless pots filled with a potting compost (soil mix). Dig a trench about 15–23cm/6–9in deep in the green-house border and line it with a waterproof plastic, to minimize soil-borne diseases.

4 Fill the trench with fine gravel, coarse grit or expanded clay granules. Then place the special bottomless ring culture pots on the aggregate base and fill them with a good loam-based potting compost (soil mix).

5 Plant into the ring and insert a cane or provide an alternative support. Water only into the ring at first. Once the plant is established and some roots have penetrated into the aggregate, water only the aggregate and feed through the pot.

6 Growing bags are less trouble than ring culture to set up, but you must feed plants regularly, and watering can be more difficult to control unless you use an automatic system. Insert a cane through the bag or use a string or spiral support.

grit or gravel in the lined trench and place special ring culture bottomless pots on top. Fill the pots with a loam-based soil mix and plant the tomatoes. Water only into the rings, but once the plants are established and some roots have penetrated the aggregate below, feed through the pot but water through the aggregate.

SUPPORTING TOMATOES ON STRINGS

When tomatoes are grown as cordons, they need some form of support, and using string is a simple and economical way to do this. Fix one wire as high as practical from one end of the greenhouse to the other, aligning it above the border, and another wire

just above the ground. The lower wire is most conveniently fixed to a stout stake at each end of the row. Tie lengths of string between the top and bottom wires, in line with each plant.

You do not need to tie the tomato plant to its support, just loop the string around the growing tip so that it forms a spiral.

MAINTENANCE

The cultivars of tomato usually grown in the greenhouse need regular attention, like the removal of sideshoots, feeding and tying in. Keep a watch, too, for early signs of pests and diseases that could reduce the quantity or quality of the crop.

Regular feeding is crucial for tomato plants to ensure constant growth and productivity. Watering is even more important as plants can very easily suffer if they are allowed to dry out, particularly if they are in containers, and this can adversely affect the quality of the tomato crop.

Plants should be watered before they show obvious signs of distress such as wilting. Feeling the potting compost is the best and most practical way to check for dryness, but this is time-consuming, especially since you should ideally feel a little way below the surface.

Moisture indicators for individual pots can be helpful for a beginner, or if there are just a few plants, but they are not a practical solution if you have a whole greenhouse or conservatory (porch) full of plants. In this case, it is well worth considering the installation of an automatic or semi-automatic watering system.

SUMMER CARE

1 If the plants are supported by strings, simply loop the string around the top of the shoot whenever necessary. It will eventually form a spiral support that holds the stem upright.

2 To secure the plant to a cane, wrap the string twice around the stake and loop it loosely around the stem before tying the knot. Do not tie the string too tight or you may damage the stem.

3 In the morning, snap off sideshoots while they are still small. They will snap off cleanly if you pull them sideways. Do not remove sideshoots if you have a low-growing bush variety.

4 If fruits are failing to form, poor pollination may be the problem. Shake the plants gently each day or spray the flowers with water to spread the pollen around.

5 The lowest leaves often turn yellow as they age. Remove these, as they will not contribute to feeding the plant, and letting more light reach the fruits can help to ripen them.

6 Stop your plants, by removing the growing tip, when they have formed as many trusses of fruit as are likely to ripen. In cold areas this may be as few as four in an unheated greenhouse.

RIGHT Some tomato feeds are high in nitrogen for early growth, but when the fruit is developing, a high-potash tomato fertilizer is best.

If the tomatoes are in pots, capillary matting is an ideal way to water them in summer. You can use a proprietary system fed by mains water, or improvise with a length of gutter for the water supply. You can keep it topped up by hand, with special water bags or from a cistern.

When you are watering by hand, use the can without a rose unless you are watering seedlings. This will enable you to direct water more easily to the roots rather than sprinkling the leaves, which might scorch. Use a finger over the end of the spout to control the flow.

An overhead sprinkler system operated automatically or when you turn on the tap is useful for a large greenhouse, either for plants

on benches or for those planted in the border. Water is not carefully directed to where it is needed, so it is not ideal for plants in pots.

DAMPING DOWN

Splashing or spraying water over the greenhouse path (known as damping down) helps to create a humid atmosphere. This is beneficial for most crops and most plants appreciate a moist atmosphere on a warm day – including the majority of pot-plants. Do it often on very hot days, to create the kind of humid atmosphere that most tropical plants prefer.

LIQUID FERTILIZERS

The best method of feeding tomatoes is with a liquid fertilizer. There are several brands that have been specifically designed for use with tomatoes. In most cases there

is sufficient fertilizer in growing bags to last until the plants start fruiting and it is at this stage that liquid fertilizer is used. Check the manufacturer's instructions and follow them carefully.

ABOVE Liquid fertilizer, diluted with water, is a quick way of feeding tomatoes.

ABOVE Spraying water on a greenhouse path creates a humid atmosphere.

Growing tomatoes outside

Tomatoes are perennials in very warm climates but are grown as annuals elsewhere. They are half-hardy and can be grown under glass or outside. Crops grown outside often taste better, especially if the summer has been hot and the fruit has ripened well. They can either be grown on cordons (upright plants) or as bushes.

PLANTING OUT

When cordons are grown outdoors the plants must be hardened off before they are planted out. Wait until there is very little risk of frost, about the same time as you plant tender summer bedding plants in late spring or early summer.

Choose varieties recommended for outdoors. They should be placed in an open, sunny position and in fertile soil, about 30–60cm/ 12–24in apart, depending on the cultivar. Some tall, indeterminate varieties can reach about 2m/7ft and need to be cordoned off the ground by staking, trellising, by growing them up strings or special metal spirals. The sideshoots that grow between the main stem and the leaves are pinched out when they are about 5–8cm/2–3in long.

BUSH TOMATOES

Determinate or bush varieties are treated in the same way, except that there is no need to remove the

CULTIVATION OUTDOORS

Sowing time inside: mid-spring
Planting-out time: early summer
Planting distance (cordon):
   45cm/18in
Planting distance (bush):
   60cm/24in
Distance between rows: 75cm/30in
Harvesting: late summer onwards

sideshoots or stake them. These are normally grown in the open garden, unlike most cordons, which can be grown either inside or out.

Whereas sideshoots are removed from cordons as they appear, leaving just the central stem, they are left in place on bush varieties, so that the plants become spreading. Because they grow more densely than cordon forms, they need to be planted further apart, in order that plenty of air can circulate around the prostrate plants.

Once the fruit begins to form, the weight on the branches increases and they usually touch the ground. This means that the tomatoes can get rather muddy. The plants will benefit from a straw mulch, which will keep the fruit off the soil and keep moisture in the soil.

Slugs and snails find it easy to get at the low fruit and so counter-measures must be taken to prevent

LEFT Cordon tomatoes should be well supported. These special spirals support the plants without the necessity of tying them.

ABOVE Pinch or cut out the sideshoots on cordon tomatoes.

LEFT Two or three tomato plants can be grown in the compost (soil mix) in a growing bag. It is important to feed them regularly.

this. Go out at night with a torch (flashlight) and collect as many as you can find. Apart from the above, bush tomatoes can be treated in the same way as cordon varieties, especially with regard to watering, feeding and protecting fruit.

USING GROWING BAGS

It is very easy to grow tomatoes without open beds of soil. Growing bags can be placed anywhere and are ideal for placing on patios or along a wide path. They are best placed against a sunny wall, which

will also act as a support for tying canes or strings so that winds do not spoil the plants. They are treated the same way as inside greenhouses, except that they are not planted until after the frosts have finished.

PLANTING OUT

1 Plant at the spacing recommended for the variety – some grow tall and large, others remain small and compact. Always make sure they have been hardened off.

2 In cold areas, cover plants with cloches for a few weeks or use horticultural fleece.

3 Once the fleece or protection has been removed, stake the plants immediately. Some small varieties may not require staking.

WATERING AND FEEDING

Outdoor tomatoes demand less attention than greenhouse varieties, especially if you grow the determinate or bush varieties. Feeding and watering is a necessary routine if you want a good crop of quality fruits. Regular watering not only ensures a heavy crop but also reduces the risk of fruit splitting through uneven watering. This sometimes happens if dry weather produces hard skins, which then cannot cope with a sudden spurt of growth following a wet period.

Add a liquid fertilizer to the water, at the rate and frequency recommended by the manufacturer. How well your tomatoes crop out-doors depends on a combination of variety, care and climate. In cold areas, outdoor tomatoes can be a disappointing crop, in warm areas you will almost certainly have more fruit than you can cope with.

PROTECTING TOMATOES

In early autumn, green tomatoes can be ripened indoors provided they have reached a reasonable stage of maturity, but it makes sense to ripen as many as possible on the plant. As soon as a severe frost is forecast, however, harvest the remaining fruit and ripen as many as possible indoors.

Fleece can also be used to protect cordon tomatoes while still staked. Sheets of fleece can be wrapped around, or you may be able to buy fleece produced as a tube. Simply cut off the required length, slip it over the plant, and secure at the top and bottom.

TOMATOES IN THE BORDER

This is the best method of growing tomatoes for the beginner or anyone else who finds watering a chore. The plants will have a lot more space for their roots to roam, so they will be less dependent on

you for food and water. You will need to improve the soil with well-rotted organic matter before planting and to incorporate a general fertilizer at the rate recommended by the manufacturer. You will still need to water the plants thoroughly every couple of days during the height of summer as this is important for tasty crops.

The main drawback of border planting is that soil-borne pests and diseases can build up after a few years, so once every few years it is a good idea to dig out the soil and replace it with fresh soil from a different part of the garden.

RIPENING AND HARVESTING

The end of the season usually comes before all the fruit has ripened. Indoor cherry varieties are normally the first to bear fruit and ripen and the long-vine types take longer. In late summer, the top of the main stem can be pruned back

SUMMER MAINTENANCE

1 If growing a cordon variety (one that you grow as a single main stem, supported by a cane), keep removing sideshoots as they develop in the junction between the stem and the leaf.

2 Regular tying to the support is even more important outdoors than in the greenhouse, as strong winds can break an untied stem and shorten the productive life of the plant. Use soft string or special twist ties.

3 As soon as the plant has set the number of trusses (sprays) of fruit likely to be ripened in your area, pinch out the top of the plant. In many areas you can only really expect to ripen four trusses, but in warm areas it may be more.

1 Frost will kill tomatoes, but you can often extend their season by a few weeks and ripen a few more fruits on the plant with protection. Bush plants that are already low growing are best covered with a large cloche. Packing straw beneath the plants first will also provide a little insulation.

2 Cordon-trained tomatoes must be lowered before they can be protected with cloches. Untie the plant and remove the stake. Be careful not to break its stem as you lower it.

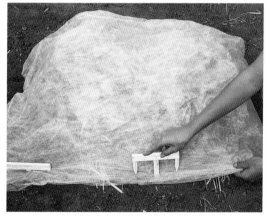

3 Lay a bed of straw on the ground, then carefully lower the plants on to this. If you lay all the stems in the same direction, you will have a neat row of tomatoes that are easily covered with a line of cloches. A long tunnel of polythene (plastic) is also suitable.

4 Fleece can be used to offer wind protection and enough shelter to keep off a degree or two of frost, though it does not warm the air during the day in the same way as glass or some rigid plastics. Drape several layers over low-growing varieties and peg it down along each side and at the ends.

to stop new growth and encourage the fruits to mature and ripen. You can also dig up the whole cordon or bush and hang it upside down in a greenhouse or frost-free shed so that the last ones ripen. Alternatively, cut down the plant from its support, lay it on a bed of straw and cover with a cloche.

Growing tomatoes in containers

Increasing interest is being shown in containers as a method of growing a few tomatoes in a small space, perhaps on the patio or possibly even on a balcony or roof garden. There is a range of beautiful containers now available from garden centres and nurseries that are suitable for tomatoes.

TYPES OF CONTAINERS

Virtually any container can be used to grow tomatoes, but success is more likely if it is reasonably large – the bigger the better, in fact. Most vegetables do not like to dry out and the greater the volume of compost (soil mix) that is available to the plant's roots, the less chance there is of this occurring.

Terracotta pots are extremely attractive, but the porous nature of the material allows water to evaporate more quickly through the sides of the pot than through, say, a glazed or plastic one. Most pots are heavy even without compost (soil mix), so make sure you position them before you fill them. Large, black plastic buckets are practical and can be used successfully, although they are not as attractive as ceramic pots. Make sure that any container you use has as least one drainage hole in the base to prevent waterlogging.

HANGING BASKETS

Generally, hanging baskets are not ideal for growing large crops of tomatoes, mainly because they are too small and the plant will become very heavy when the fruits appear, but a basket can be very eye-catching. Some cultivars of tomato are trailing, producing tiny, bite-size fruit, and these are suitable for baskets. A little imagination should allow you to create something productive as well as attractive.

ABOVE Some varieties of tomato, such as 'Tumbler', have been specially bred for use in hanging baskets. They can look as good as conventional ornamental plants.

The 'Tumbler' tomato variety is compact but heavy-fruiting and has been bred especially for use in containers, window boxes and hanging baskets. Plant them in spring or early summer in a greenhouse until midsummer and then move outside to a sunny, sheltered position. Keep the tomato plants watered at all times, and feed with a proprietary tomato food or liquid seaweed.

LEFT Tomatoes combine well with herbs. Here, they have been planted with both green and purple basil.

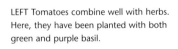

RIGHT Plum tomatoes ripening on the
vine have an enticing aroma as well as
their luscious taste.

'Totem' tomatoes are good
choices for containers. They grow
to only 25cm/10in in height and
spread, but bear heavy crops.

POSITION

You will have to choose where you
site your containers carefully. Select
a warm but not hot place, such as a
patio, preferably one where there is
plenty of fresh air circulating, but
where the tomatoes are not
exposed to strong winds.

Tomatoes grown in pots do not
have the solid mass of earth around
their roots to keep them cool
during the day and it is possible
that the roots can become too hot.
Containers of tomatoes should not
be grown in the shade as it is too
cold. You will need to water the
tomatoes frequently, especially on
hot days when they may need
several waterings. Grow tomatoes
amongst herbs, such as basil, to
help deter insects and pests.

GROWING BAGS

The main container used by most
gardeners for tomatoes is the
growing bag. It is simply a
plastic bag filled with a specially
formulated compost. There is
nothing elegant about it, but it
does serve its purpose very well.
However, growing bags can be

LEFT 'Tumbler' tomatoes have been
planted at even spaces along the centre
of this window box.

effectively disguised. Bush varieties
will soon flop over the plastic and
hide it. It is possible to buy special
containers that will hold one or
more bags, or you can make one
yourself from wood. They can,
for example, be placed in large
wooden troughs, or the bags can
be disguised by growing marigolds
in them as well, which will soon
cover the plastic. Special supports
can be purchased that fit round
the bag to hold taller varieties.

Harvesting and storing

The great moment comes when the tomatoes are ready to harvest; nothing tastes quite like fresh fruit and vegetables that you have grown for yourself. However, not all the produce can be eaten at once and it is prudent to store some or make tomato sauces, pastes and chutneys, especially for the winter months.

RIPENING

Home-grown tomatoes are best for flavour and they are at their peak when they have ripened naturally in the sun. They should ideally be allowed to ripen slowly on the plant so that their flavour can fully develop and they have a good aroma, not only from the green stalks, but also from the tomato itself. Red tomatoes should be deep red. Yellow or orange tomatoes should also have good depth of colour. The fruit should have flesh that is firm, but gives slightly when pressed gently.

ABOVE Harvest tomatoes when they are ripe, which will usually be when they turn red. Leave the stalk on.

Leave slightly hard tomatoes to ripen at room temperature and preferably in direct sunlight. Paler tomatoes or those tinged with green will redden if kept in a brown paper bag or fruit bowl with a ripe tomato or banana; the gases given off will ripen the tomatoes, although they cannot improve the basic flavour. Ripening on the plant is the only way to ensure a really sweet taste, which is largely why commercial tomatoes are so often inferior. Overripe tomatoes, where the skin has split and they are bursting with juice, are good in soups and sauces.

LEFT At the end of the season, dig up any remaining plants and hang them upside down under protection to ripen.

However, check for any sign of mould or decay, as this would spoil the flavour of the finished product.

HARVESTING

Try to resist the temptation to harvest tomatoes too soon. Indoor cherry tomatoes are the first to bear fruit, whereas long-vine types take longer. Until they have developed fully, the taste might not be matured and some might even be bitter. When you are harvesting do not simply pick the best fruits. If you also come across any that are diseased or rotting, harvest these as

RIGHT In a good year, you should have plenty of tomatoes to preserve in sauces and chutneys for winter.

well and compost them. Do not leave rotting tomatoes on the plant or on the ground because they will spread their problems to healthy fruit or the spores may remain in the ground until the following year.

There is no hard-and-fast rule about when or at what time of day to harvest, although taking the tomato straight from the garden to the pot does, of course, give the freshest tasting dish. If possible, try to harvest when you want the tomatoes, rather than leaving them lying around for a few days.

STORING

There are several ways of storing tomatoes for later use. If you pick one and are unable to use it right away, it can usually be kept a few

days before use. The best way of keeping these is to store them in a cool, dark place, preferably a cellar or cold shed. However, this is not always possible and a refrigerator is the next best thing. The important thing about storing fruits and vegetables is that they should not

LEFT 'Gardener's Delight' growing with the companion herb basil.

touch one another and that air should be able to circulate freely around them. Tomatoes can be frozen but then they can only be used in cooked dishes as they lose their firmness.

Another traditional way to store tomatoes, frequently used by Italians, is to make sun-dried tomatoes. These can then be preserved in olive oil for future use.

Growing tomatoes organically

As increasing numbers of people become concerned about the levels of artificial insecticides, fungicides and weedkillers used in the commercial production of all vegetables and fruit, the attractions of organically grown produce are becoming self-evident. Tomatoes are an ideal crop to grow organically, whether you grow them in the garden or in a greenhouse or conservatory (porch).

ORGANIC GARDENS

There is more to organic gardening than just not using chemicals. Organic gardeners work to improve the quality of the soil to provide plants with the best possible growing conditions. They also aim to develop a natural balance within the garden by attracting wildlife to help combat pests and to pollinate plants, and by growing a wide range of plants. In this way attacks by pests and diseases affect only a small proportion of the entire vegetable plot and the inclusion of companion plants acts as a positive deterrent to some forms of pest.

In the vegetable garden do not plant tomatoes with potatoes and kohl rabi, because these plants are susceptible to many of the same diseases and predators. Instead,

RIGHT The French marigolds planted with a row of tomatoes in this bed will ward off potential pests, especially whitefly. This is known as companion planting.

plant tomatoes near to asparagus, basil, carrots, parsley, onions and garlic. Including clumps of French marigolds (*Tagetes*), which have a distinctive, pungent scent, in the vegetable garden has been shown to have a useful deterrent effect on aphids.

Rather than single or double digging the vegetable plot on a regular basis, some organic gardeners prefer the no-dig system. After an initial thorough digging to remove all perennial weed roots and other debris, the soil is gradually built up by the annual addition of mulches of well-rotted compost and manure. Worms and soil-borne organisms take the nutrients down into the soil; the gardener does not dig in the material. Because the ground is not disturbed by digging, the soil is not unnecessarily aerated (which increases the rate at which nutrients can leach out) and the natural layers of soil that develop over time are not destroyed. No-dig beds are usually found as raised beds or as areas of the vegetable garden that are surrounded by permanent or semi-permanent paths so that the soil is never compacted.

FERTILIZING THE SOIL

In addition to regular applications of well-rotted compost or manure, organic gardeners often sow green manures in ground that has become vacant as a crop is cleared after harvesting. These plants, which include alfalfa, some types of beans and peas and *Phacelia tanacetifolia*, are dug into the

RIGHT Tomatoes growing organically in the border with pots of herbs nearby.

ground before they have set seed and are valuable for fixing nitrogen in the soil.

One of the most useful and decorative green manures is a pretty hardy annual, the poached-egg plant (*Limnanthes douglasii*), which can be sown in autumn (when the tomatoes have been cleared away) and will produce a good weed-suppressing ground cover of leaves, which can be dug in the following spring, before the flowers appear. The flowers are useful for attracting beneficial hoverflies and bees to the garden. They will also self-seed readily.

Tomato plants are greedy feeders, and when they are in containers or growing bags they will need additional food. Liquid seaweed extract is excellent, or you can make your own liquid feed.

The perennial Russian comfrey (*Symphytum* x *uplandicum*) is a vigorous plant that can be grown to produce a liquid feed. Once established, plants can be cut back several times a year. The nitrogen- and potassium-rich leaves can be added to the compost heap as an activator or allowed to decay in water to form a smelly but potash-rich feed, which is ideal for tomatoes. Although not as attractive as comfrey, nettle leaves (*Urtica dioica*) can also be used to make a good liquid feed, which contains magnesium, sulphur and iron. Young nettle leaves are also useful compost activators.

BIOLOGICAL CONTROLS

If you are growing tomatoes in a greenhouse you will find that any predators that do appear will thrive in the protected environment. It is not just organic gardeners who prefer not to spray greenhouse crops with insecticides and other chemicals. Biological controls, which are increasingly widely available, are the ideal way of controlling many common pests. They usually work best when the weather is warm, although some are not suitable for outdoor use.

Introduce them as soon as the first signs of attack are noticed, and do not use any insecticides at all once a biological control has been introduced. Be patient and accept that there will be some damage before the biological agent takes effect. When you use biological controls there will always be some pests – they are essential for the predator to continue to breed – but the population will be reduced, and damage should be negligible.

Pests and diseases

Although the list of potential pests and diseases that can affect tomatoes may be off-putting, you will be unfortunate if your plants suffer from more than the odd infestation of whitefly. Check your plants regularly to look for early signs of disease or insects and take the appropriate action before it becomes serious. Many problems can be avoided altogether by making sure that your plants are well watered and fed and that there is plenty of air circulating around them. Good hygiene in the greenhouse is essential. Remove all dead and dying foliage regularly, and at the end of the year give the entire structure and all pots, containers and staging a thorough clean with hot, soapy water.

APHIDS

Blackfly and greenfly (and other colours) suck the sap of a plant, weakening it, checking the growth and often transmitting viral diseases. Various species of black aphid are attracted to the new, soft growth of tomato plants.

If you wish to use chemicals choose a selective insecticide, such as one containing pirimicarb, which will kill the aphids but not other, beneficial insects. Organic insecticides include pyrethrum, derris and insecticidal soaps. The larvae of a species of gall midge,

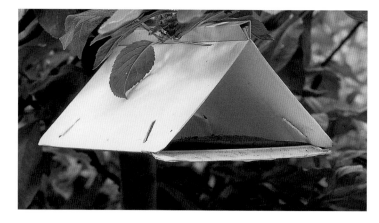

ABOVE Biological controls are a good way to fight pests and are mainly used in greenhouses. The control insects are released, here from a sachet, to attack the pests.

Aphidoletes aphidomyza, feed on aphids and can be introduced as a biological control in the greenhouse. Outdoors, encourage natural predators, such as ladybirds (ladybugs) and hoverflies by growing yarrow and pot marigolds.

BLOSSOM END ROT

A round, dark brown, sunken patch appears at the blossom end (base) of affected tomatoes. The cause is lack of calcium in the fruit, and this is, in turn, the result of inadequate or irregular watering; it is a particular problem of plants in

LEFT Sticky traps are a form of non-spray control that is becoming popular for a range of pests. Here, pheromones attract insect pests to the trap, where they get stuck. Other traps consist of pieces of yellow plastic covered with a non-drying glue.

GLASSHOUSE WHITEFLY

The leaves of plants are covered with minute white insects, which fly up into the air when they are disturbed. The undersides of leaves are usually covered with greenish-white scales. Honeydew and sooty mould may also be present.

If you don't mind using chemicals, spray with pyrethrum, bifenthrin or permethrin. Organic gardeners will use sticky yellow traps (plastic cards covered with non-drying glue) to check whether whitefly are present. The traps may be sufficient to control a small number of insects, and many more can be sucked up with a portable vacuum cleaner.

Insecticidal soap can be used to control infestations, but more reliable are parasitic wasps (*Encarsia formosa*). Do not introduce the wasps if you have used pesticides during the previous two months, nor if there are no whitefly present. Do not use the wasps before the night-time temperature is about

containers or growing bags. Affected fruits will not recover and should be removed and discarded. Water regularly to avoid the problem.

BOTRYTIS

Also known as grey mould, this is a particular problem in humid, poorly ventilated greenhouses. It can also affect plants that have soft growth or have been wounded when sideshoots were cut off. Leaves, stems and sometimes whole plants are covered with a greyish-brown, velvety mould. Remove yellowing or decaying leaves as soon as you notice them and pick off all overripe fruit to avoid infection. Good ventilation and watering early in the morning (not in the evening) will help. If necessary, fumigate the greenhouse at the end of the season with tecnazene smokes.

DAMPING OFF

Seedlings are sometimes affected by damping off, a rapidly spreading fungal problem that causes their roots to rot, leading to the collapse of the entire plantlet. A fluffy growth can be seen on the

seedlings and, sometimes, on the surface of the compost. If seedlings are affected there is no cure. Prevent the problem by avoiding overwatering, providing adequate ventilation and maintaining good greenhouse hygiene. Water with a weak solution of a copper-based fungicide from time to time.

FUNGAL DISEASES

A number of fungal diseases, leading to foot and root rots, will cause plants to wilt and foliage to turn yellow. Planting in moisture-retentive but well-drained soil and adopting crop rotation outdoors will ensure that plants withstand most diseases. Badly affected plants should be removed and destroyed.

GHOST SPOT

Small spots, each surrounded by a lighter ring, appear on the fruit. This is a fungal disease, which can be avoided if you make sure that you do not splash water on the fruit when you are damping down the greenhouse or watering.

RIGHT Whitefly are minute white insects.

15°C/59°F, and remove all yellow sticky traps before introducing the wasps. *Encarsia formosa* larvae are supplied on cards, which are suspended from the plants. The wasps emerge from the cards and parasitize the whitefly. Do not remove any leaves that have black scales on the undersides: these are the wasps. Planting French marigolds (*Tagetes*) nearby may also help to deter whitefly.

GREENBACK

When tomatoes are grown under glass the fruits sometimes develop a ring of leathery, darker tissue around the shoulder at the stalk end. Although the rest of the plant will continue to grow normally, the affected fruit will not ripen properly, remaining green or sometimes turning yellow.

This is caused by insufficient potassium or phosphorus, but it can also be the result of too high temperatures and sun scorch. Make sure that the developing fruits are adequately shaded – never remove the leaves above a developing truss – and improve the ventilation in the greenhouse to maintain an even temperature.

MAGNESIUM DEFICIENCY

The lower leaves develop orange-yellow patches between the veins; if nothing is done, upper leaves are also affected. This can be a problem in wet weather, especially if tomatoes are being grown on sandy soil. The condition is made worse by waterlogging and compacted soil.

RIGHT Red spider mites produce a distinctive webbing of fine white silk.

Organic gardeners can apply a foliar feed of a weak solution of Epsom salts at fortnightly intervals. A longer-term solution is to reduce the use of potassium fertilizer and, if the soil pH is appropriate, to add dolomitic limestone.

PITH NECROSIS

This bacterial problem causes the top leaves to wilt and turn yellow just as the fruits begin to ripen. The stems develop dark brown, dry patches. All infected plants should be removed and destroyed.

POTATO BLIGHT

This disease of potatoes also affects tomatoes. Brownish patches appear on the leaves and the stems may collapse. A dry, brownish rot may develop on the fruit, although this may not become apparent until after picking.

Remove and destroy any infected plants and spray unaffected plants with a copper-based fungicide or mancozeb. Organically, in the greenhouse there is little that can be done except to reduce its spread by improving ventilation. Spraying with Bordeaux mixture will protect plants if used early in the season, but it will have little effect in wet weather.

POTATO CYST EELWORM

There are no chemicals available to amateur gardeners to control this soil-dwelling pest, which lives in the roots of potatoes and tomatoes and causes yellow and stunted growth. Crop rotation will help avoid infestation.

RED SPIDER MITE

This can be a serious problem of tomatoes grown under glass, causing the leaves to turn yellowish and die. Colonies of greenish mites (they are only red in autumn and winter) can be seen with a magnifying glass on the undersides of the leaves. Heavily infested plants will have a tell-tale webbing of fine white silk between the leaves and the stems.

Spray the undersides of the leaves with bifenthrin, pirimiphos-methyl or dimethoate at intervals, following the directions on the packet for timing, quantity and frequency of repeat applications. The organic solutions are to improve the plants' growing conditions by making sure that the soil does not dry out and that the atmosphere is kept moist by regular misting. You can also introduce the predatory mite *Phytoseiulus persimilis* when the daytime temperature is above 21°C/70°F.

SLUGS AND SNAILS

Tomatoes in the garden may be eaten by slugs and snails, which can do untold damage. There are many ways of ridding the garden of them, including using containers of beer sunk into the beds, but even more effective is to go out at night with a torch (flashlight) and to pick up by hand as many as you can see. Kill them by putting them in salty water, or release them on waste ground. Alternatively, surround individual plants with heaps of grit. If you must, you can use slug baits, but always clear away the dead slugs and snails so that they are not eaten by birds. Biological controls, which involve watering nematodes into warm, damp soil, will help to reduce the numbers of soil-living slugs, but they are ineffective against the larger slugs and most snails. Plants in containers can be protected by the use of copper tape.

SPLIT FRUITS

Irregular watering, such as may happen when a downpour follows a period of drought and causes a spurt of growth, can cause fruit to split. Improving the water-retentive character of the soil by digging in plenty of well-rotted compost or manure will help to reduce the risk to outdoor tomatoes. In the greenhouse, water regularly.

TOBACCO MOSAIC VIRUS

Mottled leaves, reduced vigour and poor setting can be caused by a number of viruses, including tobacco mosaic virus. Destroy affected plants and do not use the soil for tomatoes again. Choose virus-resistant cultivars.

TOMATO LEAF MOULD

Plants in greenhouses or polythene tunnels sometimes develop a brownish-purple mould on the undersides of the leaves and yellow blotches on the upper surfaces. Botrytis (see above) may follow. Choose resistant cultivars and try to keep the temperature in the greenhouse below 21°C/70°F. Make sure the greenhouse is well ventilated because the problem is worse in high humidity. Spray with carbendazim or mancozeb (following the manufacturer's instructions) and make sure that the greenhouse is thoroughly cleaned at the end of the season.

TOMATO STEM ROT

This will cause mature plants to wilt suddenly. A dark brown canker will develop on the stem at ground

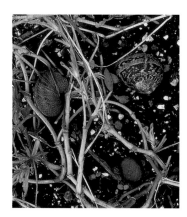

LEFT Snails can demolish large quantities of young growth.

ABOVE Vine weevil larvae.

level, and small black specks (fungal spores) can be seen on affected leaves and stems. The spores will overwinter in the ground, so infected plants must be removed and destroyed.

VINE WEEVILS

These insects pose an increasing problem, especially to container-grown plants. The adults eat notches in the edges of leaves, but the real damage is done by the creamy-white, C-shaped larvae, which live in the compost and eat root systems, causing plants to collapse. The most reliable control is to water in nematodes, or micro-scopic eelworms, in late summer or early autumn when the soil is moist but still warm. Plants in containers can be protected by using non-set glue to stop the adult weevils climbing into the pots.

WEEDKILLER DAMAGE

Even in the best organic gardens spray drift of hormone weedkillers or residue on straw or grass clippings used as a mulch will cause leaves to be narrow and twisted, and stems may grow in a spiral. If fruit appears it may be hollow and seedless.

Index